SANTA FE PUBLIC LIBRARY

WITHI

D0604283

MC
E

GIRAFFES

BY JUDITH JANGO-COHEN

BENCHMARK BOOKS

MARSHALL CAVENDISH
NEW YORK

For my sister Regina, who, like the giraffe, is beautiful and has a big heart.
— J. J. C.

Series Consultant:
James Doherty
General Curator
The Bronx Zoo, New York

Benchmark Books
Marshall Cavendish Corporation
99 White Plains Road
Tarrytown, NY 10591–9001
Website: www.marshallcavendish.us

Copyright 2002 by Judith Jango-Cohen

All rights reserved. No part of this book may be reproduced or utilized in any form or by any means electronic or mechanical including photocopying, recording, or by any information storage and retrieval system, without permission from the copyright holders.

Library of Congress Cataloging-in-Publication Data
Jango-Cohen, Judith.
Giraffes / by Judith Jango-Cohen.
p. cm. – (Animals, animals)
ISBN 0-7614-1258-1
1. Giraffes—Juvenile literature. [1. Giraffe.] I. Title. II. Series.

QL737.U56 J36 2001   599.638—dc21   00-052323

Cover photo: Courtesy of *McDonald Wildlife Photography* © Mary Ann McDonald

All photographs are used by permission and through the courtesy of: *Animals Animals:* Johnny Johnson: 8; Len Rue, Jr.: 11 (right); Willard Luce, 17; D. Allen: 20, 31; Betty K. Bruce: 22, 28; Betty H. Press: 24; Zig Leszczynski, 34; Arthur Gloor, 36; D. Balfour, 43; © *Michael Burgess*, 38; *ENP Images:* Gerry Ellis, 13; © *Randall Hyman:* 18; © *Tom and Pat Leeson:* 14, 32; *McDonald Wildlife Photography* © Mary Ann McDonald: 4; *Visuals Unlimited, Inc.:* Ken Lucas, 10; John Cunningham: 11 (left); Mark Newman, 26;

Printed in China

3   5   6   4

CONTENTS

1
INTRODUCING GIRAFFES

Long ago, a "strangely shaped animal of a wonderful kind" was captured and paraded before a king. Its marvelous appearance astounded everyone. The head was almost twice as large as that of an ostrich, the neck was long and slender like a swan's, its skin was marked with spots like a leopard's, and its size was about that of a camel.

This is how an ancient Greek writer described an animal that he called camelopardalis, which means a camel's body with a leopard's coat. People still call it this today–if they are scientists. The animal's common name is giraffe. Some language experts think *giraffe* comes from a word meaning "assemblage," or a putting together of animals.

Two thousand years ago, giraffes were unknown to

THE *JUST SO STORIES*, BY RUDYARD KIPLING, TELL US THAT THE GIRAFFE GOT ITS "BLOTCHY" SPOTS BY HIDING IN THE "SLIPPERY-SLIDY SHADOWS OF THE TREES . . ."

most Europeans. They got their first look at one when the emperor, Julius Caesar, brought a giraffe to Rome in 46 B.C.

African people have been painting and carving pictures of giraffes for over five thousand years. African earth holds ancient giraffe fossils. It is on African grass-lands called *savannas* that giraffes are at home. Their splotchy coat blends with the sun-speckled leaves, and their long limbs hide among the trunks of trees.

The legs of a full-grown giraffe are taller than the average person—about six feet (1.8 m). On these sturdy stilts giraffes can cover fifteen feet (4.5 m) in one stride. To walk, they lift both left legs, and then both right. Giraffes stroll like this at about ten miles per hour (16 km), which means that a person would have to jog to keep up. A running giraffe can easily outpace a person, or even a horse, reaching a top speed of up to thirty-five miles (56 km) per hour. When galloping, a giraffe's hind legs move ahead and outside of its front ones, so its limbs do not get tangled. Although they can move fast, giraffes run out of breath quickly. It is hard work to move air up and down a six-foot (1.8-m) windpipe.

Giraffe Skeleton

The long neck of the giraffe has only seven vertebrae, the same as other mammals. The difference is that each of a giraffe's vertebra is enlarged and has ball–and–socket joints that give it greater flexibility.

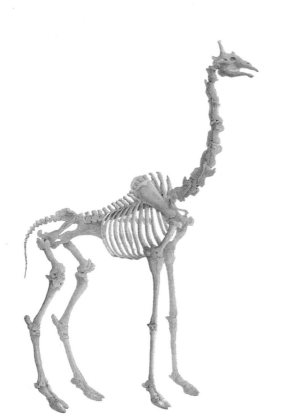

An adult male giraffe may stand up to eighteen feet (5.4 m) high. The okapi, on the other hand, is considerably smaller at a maximum height of seven feet (2.15 m).

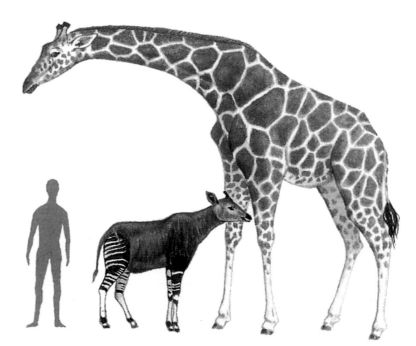

ON OPEN SAVANNAS, GIRAFFES
CAN FIND A PREDATOR BEFORE
IT FINDS THEM.

8

To avoid toppling over, this tallest of land animals balances on big feet. Each heavy hoof is about the size of a Frisbee. The forefeet are a bit larger than the hind ones. Because their feet are encased in hard hoofs, giraffes are called *ungulates.* Other ungulates are deer, pigs, cattle, and camels. The only other ungulate in the giraffe family (Giraffidae) is the zebra–sized okapi. These animals have a short neck and striped legs.

THE OKAPI IS THE ONLY LIVING RELATIVE OF THE GIRAFFE. THIS TIMID RAIN FOREST CREATURE WAS DISCOVERED BY EUROPEAN EXPLORERS IN ABOUT 1900.

THE RETICULATED GIRAFFE OF EAST AFRICA IS THE SUBSPECIES MOST OFTEN SEEN IN ZOOS.

ALL MASAI GIRAFFES HAVE SIMILAR JAGGED SKIN PATTERNS, BUT EACH GIRAFFE'S COAT DESIGN IS UNIQUE.

Scientists divide the giraffe *species* into eight groups, or subspecies, based on their markings. Two subspecies in East Africa are the reticulated giraffe, with straight-edged, blocky spots, and the Masai giraffe, which wears a delicate leafy design.

Giraffe subspecies are different not only in their markings, but in the number of knobs on their heads. These bony bumps, called *exostoses*, are covered with skin and capped with wiry, black hair. All giraffes have at least two exostoses, but males may have from three to five, depending on the subspecies. What do males do with these bumpy heads? They battle!

2
SURVIVAL ON
THE SAVANNA

One warm morning, two young male giraffes are peacefully nibbling on leafy branches. Then, without warning, the taller one stops eating and slowly bends back his neck. Thud! His bony head slams against the other's back. Soon both giraffes start swinging their heads. They also wrestle with their strong necks, wrapping them around each other.

After a while they stop banging, begin rubbing necks, and go back to eating, as if nothing had happened. Male giraffes often play–fight like this. These *necking* games help them see who is larger and stronger. The winner of these matches will become the *dominant* male. He will be the leader, mating with his choice of females.

YOUNG MALE GIRAFFES PRACTICE NECKING. THIS PREPARES THEM FOR MORE SERIOUS CONTESTS WHEN THEY ARE OLDER.

LIONS DO NOT HAVE A
CHANCE OF SNEAKING
UP ON A HERD OF
ALERT GIRAFFES.

If a new male joins the herd and challenges the dominant bull, more serious battles are fought. The giraffes hammer each other with their heavy heads armed with nine-inch (24 cm) exostoses. One grand slam can lift a giraffe off its feet. The battle usually breaks up when one bull decides he has had too much, and walks away.

Like the males, female giraffes form their own herds. Females and their young may travel in pairs or in groups with as many as seventy-five members. Even though they may be scattered a mile apart they have no trouble seeing each other. Giraffes have the largest eyes of any land animal. They are located on the sides of their heads so giraffes can see in many directions at once.

Giraffes use their extraordinary eyesight not only to keep in touch with each other but to watch for predators. Giraffes usually stick to the open savannas where their view is not blocked. The sight of rustling grass could mean the approach of a lion. A giraffe's startled snort warns other giraffes, as well as grazing zebras and wildebeest. Together they stampede to safety.

A MALE GIRAFFE'S
BONY HEAD CAN
WEIGH ABOUT
TWENTY-FOUR
POUNDS, WHILE
A FEMALE'S WEIGHS
ABOUT EIGHT.

ZEBRAS, WILDEBEEST, AND OSTRICHES FIND THE WATCH-FUL GIRAFFE TO BE A HELPFUL COMPANION.

. . .

A GIRAFFE'S FRONT LEGS ARE MUCH LONGER THAN ITS HIND LEGS . . . RIGHT? TO FIND OUT, LOOK AT A GIRAFFE'S LEGS WHILE COVERING UP THE TOP PART OF THE PICTURE. WHAT DO YOU THINK? ACTUALLY, THE FRONT LEGS ARE JUST A LITTLE BIT LONGER. THE HIND LEGS ONLY LOOK A LOT SHORTER BECAUSE OF THE SLOPE OF THE GIRAFFE'S BACK.

. . .

Lions are the main *predators* of adult giraffes, but even they have difficulty stalking them. Sometimes lions succeed if the giraffe's view is blocked, or if its head is down while drinking. Some deeply scarred giraffes have survived lion attacks. They may have shaken a lion off by galloping through tall bushes or kicking with their hind legs.

A giraffe's legs are mighty weapons against even the fiercest lion. They are over six feet (1.8m) long, packed with heavy bone and muscle, and are shod with huge hoofs. One well-placed, powerful kick can kill or disable a lion. Unless it can sneak up on one, lions will not tangle with a healthy adult giraffe.

Lions do have some luck however, with sick or old giraffes. But their favorite targets are the new baby calves. Lions can smell their scent and are sometimes the first visitors after they are born.

3

GROWING UP AND UP

A mother giraffe bends over her calf, licking its face and ears. She is removing its newborn scent. The baby tries to wiggle away from her strong, black tongue. This calf is lucky because it was born in the hot afternoon, when predators like lions, leopards, and hyenas are resting in the shade.

The baby does not rest though. Shortly after it is born, it struggles to stand, stumbling and toppling over in the golden grass. The wobbly calf does not give up and is soon standing. Now it can drink! Reaching under its mother's belly, it noisily gulps her thick, creamy milk.

Soon the mother has to eat too, so she leaves her calf hidden in tall grass. When the mother

GIRAFFE MOTHERS ARE PREGNANT WITH THEIR CALVES FOR ONE YEAR AND THREE MONTHS.

THIS MOTHER GIRAFFE'S POWERFUL LEGS SHIELD HER WOBBLY CALF.

returns, she carefully checks for danger. The calf stays still until the mother nudges and licks it— her signal that it is safe to drink.

For the next few weeks the calf stays alone with its mother. Then it joins other calves in a nursery group called a *crèche*. Here the calves play together while their mothers come and go. There is usually one mother around to watch for danger. Sometimes an older "auntie" baby-sits. If a predator approaches, calves hide under their mother's belly while she stomps and kicks to chase the attacker away.

When calves first enter the crèche they are the size

If giraffes' blood vessels were built like ours, blood would flood their brains whenever they lowered their long necks. But in the veins that carry blood away from their heads, giraffes have control valves. These valves keep the blood from rushing backwards. And when they lift their heads up again, a ring of muscle slows the blood as it enters the heart.

of a tall, skinny person—about six feet (1.8 m) and 150 pounds (68 kg). In their first year, they can grow four more feet (1.2 m). After seven years, bulls may reach eighteen feet (5.5 m) and weigh three thousand pounds (1360 kg). Females are a couple of feet shorter and nearly a thousand pounds lighter.

Giraffes grow fastest in their first week. They sprout as much as an inch (2.5 cm) a day, feeding only on their mother's milk. Because they are mammals, this is their first food. By their third week they begin sampling leaves and twigs. They still sip their mother's milk though, because they cannot drink water. Their short necks do not yet reach the ground.

EVEN WITH THE PROTECTION
OF ADULTS, THREE OUT OF
FOUR BABY GIRAFFES DIE IN
THEIR FIRST YEAR.

After a year, when their necks are longer, calves begin to learn the giraffe method of drinking. Even adults cannot reach the water without a few tricks. To take a sip they must bend their knees or spread their legs while balancing their towering bodies. The calves have trouble at first, but they are very determined and practice this move until they have mastered it.

No matter how thirsty they are, giraffes never race down to the water hole. Cautiously, they study every bush, tree, and grassy patch. Then if it seems safe they approach the water.

A giraffe's neck is about twelve times as long as a person's. If a person has seven neck bones, how many do you think a giraffe has? Math won't help here. Giraffes have seven neck bones too, but theirs are much bigger. Each is about eight to ten inches (20-25 cm) long.

27

Other animals, who had been shuffling nervously, immediately dash down. They seem to be saying, "The giraffes are here. It must be all right." Even when they are down at the water, giraffes do not drink casually. They look up often between gulps, watching for lions. Drinking is a dangerous time for most animals but giraffes are lucky because they can go for a few days without drinking. This is partly because they can guzzle ten gallons (39 l) of water in one visit to the watering hole. They can also go a long time without water because the leaves they feed on contain moisture.

PREDATORS LIKE LIONS AND EVEN CROCODILES TRY TO SNEAK UP ON A GIRAFFE WHILE IT DRINKS.

4

MIGHTY APPETITES

As the sun's first rays warm the dry grass, two giraffes are munching away on an acacia tree. The acacia leaves are moist, up to seventy-four percent water, and are damp with dew. They are also guarded by thorns. To avoid getting hurt the giraffes close their slit-like nostrils. Bristly hairs protect their upper lips.

Despite the thorns, acacia leaves are giraffes' favorite food. Giraffes are not picky though, and will eat one hundred different kinds of plants. Giraffes are *browsers*—feeding on leaves, shoots, seeds, and fruits. A giraffe may eat seventy-five pounds (34 kg) of food a day, browsing mostly in the cool mornings and at dusk.

While feeding, the giraffe's eighteen-inch (46-cm) tongue slithers in and out of its mouth. Its tongue is *prehensile*—wrapping around things and grabbing them as our hands do. A giraffe may pluck single leaves with

A GIRAFFE'S THICK, RUBBERY SALIVA MAY PROTECT ITS MOUTH FROM THORNS.

its tongue, or it may pull entire branches into its mouth and scrape off the leaves with its teeth. If the branch is thorny, the giraffe snips off the piece it wants by biting with the lower front teeth against the tough upper gum pad.

Giraffes belong to a group of animals called *ruminants.* They swallow first and chew later. After they finish brows–ing, they rest in the hot sun. Soon their stomachs start to rumble as great wads of partly digested food, called *cuds,* are formed. Then there is a pop and the stomach

33

A GIRAFFE'S
TONGUE IS
TOUGH AND
COVERED WITH
ROUGH SPINES.

muscles push the cud up and into the throat. The cud can be seen sliding slowly up the giraffe's neck and then rolling into its mouth.

Back in the mouth the food gets thoroughly ground up by the giraffe's flat rear molars. Each cud is chewed about forty-four times, taking almost a minute. Then, this carefully chewed cud is swallowed and digested in a four-chambered stomach.

Giraffes may chew their cuds for hours in the midday heat or after dark. But when the air cools they return to browsing. Unfortunately, areas where giraffes can browse freely have become scarce.

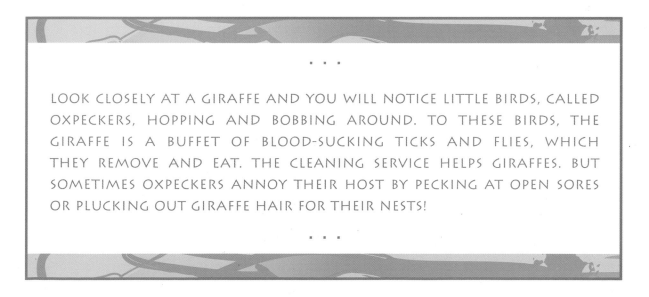

· · ·

LOOK CLOSELY AT A GIRAFFE AND YOU WILL NOTICE LITTLE BIRDS, CALLED OXPECKERS, HOPPING AND BOBBING AROUND. TO THESE BIRDS, THE GIRAFFE IS A BUFFET OF BLOOD-SUCKING TICKS AND FLIES, WHICH THEY REMOVE AND EAT. THE CLEANING SERVICE HELPS GIRAFFES. BUT SOMETIMES OXPECKERS ANNOY THEIR HOST BY PECKING AT OPEN SORES OR PLUCKING OUT GIRAFFE HAIR FOR THEIR NESTS!

· · ·

ABOUT FIFTEEN
TYPES OF TICKS
ATTACK GIRAFFES,
BUT OXPECKERS
PICK THEM OFF.

5
THE HUMAN CONNECTION

A little boy stands excitedly holding a piece of carrot in his hand. Slurp! A long, strong tongue sweeps the treat away. Another child playfully puts a carrot into her mouth. Soon she feels the giraffe's warm breath as its wet tongue grasps the snack. Other children stare into the giraffe's large, dark eyes, and stroke its silky fur.

These African boys and girls are enjoying giraffes at the Giraffe Center in Kenya. Giraffes were originally brought here in 1974 because the area where they lived was going to be set-tled by farmers. Throughout Africa, giraffe *habitat* is being changed into

THE GIRAFFE CENTER EDUCATES CHILDREN ABOUT GIRAFFES WITH A HANDS-ON APPROACH.

GIRAFFE HABITATS

 PAST HABITAT

 PRESENT HABITAT

During the 20th century, the changes to the giraffe's habitat were caused by humans. As a result of these changes, giraffes disappeared from most of western and southern Africa and are now almost completely confined to East Africa.

farmlands and factories by growing populations of people. That is why places like the Giraffe Center are so important.

Land is also set aside for giraffes in national parks and in game reserves. These areas preserve the giraffe's habitat. They also protect giraffes from *poachers*, hunters who illegally kill giraffes and other animals. Giraffes are still sometimes killed for their meat. Rangers patrol the parks, but these areas are so large that poachers are not always caught.

In the past, giraffes were hunted not only for their meat but also for their hide and hair. Their hide was prized because it is an inch (2.5 cm) thick and

. . .

GIRAFFES ARE EXTREMELY CAUTIOUS AND ARE AWARE OF EVEN SLIGHT CHANGES IN THEIR SURROUNDINGS. FOR ZOOKEEPERS THIS TRAIT CAN CAUSE HEADACHES. ONE HANDLER DISCOVERED THIS WHEN HE PLACED A SMALL TACK ON THE WALL OF A GIRAFFE STALL. WHEN THE GIRAFFES RETURNED, THEY REFUSED TO ENTER THE STALL UNTIL SOME-ONE FIGURED OUT WHY AND REMOVED THE TACK.

. . .

extremely tough, yet lightweight. It was used to make boots, drums, shields, buckets, and thirty-foot ox whips. The wiry hairs on their tails were woven into good luck bracelets or necklaces, and the tails themselves were valued as flyswatters.

Of course, people also hunted the giraffe for sport. But for many hunters, the experience left them feeling regretful. They couldn't stop thinking about how the giraffe had faced them in a quiet, dignified manner. Many also mentioned that they had looked into the giraffe's eyes and noticed tears trickling down its long lashes.

In 1890, a former hunter, Sir Samuel Baker, described his feelings: "[Giraffes] have always appeared to me the most harmless creatures that exist. They never . . . attack any animals or man, but they simply enjoy themselves in their harmless manner . . ." No doubt we could learn a lesson from this powerful but peaceful giant.

LIKE MANY OTHER AFRICAN ANIMALS, GIRAFFES NEED OUR INVOLVE-MENT TO PROTECT THEM AND THEIR HOMES.

browser: an animal that eats plant material such as leaves, fruits, flowers, and seeds, but usually not grass

crèche: a group of calves, mothers, and sometimes a baby-sitting "auntie"

cud: wad of partly digested plant material that is brought up from the first stomach chamber to be chewed again

dominant: usually the strongest and largest male who gets first pick of mates and food

exostoses: on a giraffe, bumps covered with skin and hair that start as soft tissue then harden into bone and fuse to the head

habitat: the natural surroundings, or environment, where an animal lives

necking: a contest between males in which they hit and push against each other with their heads and necks to see who is stronger

poacher: a person who illegally hunts and kills an animal

predator: an animal that hunts and eats other animals

prehensile: able to grasp or wrap around something

ruminant: an animal that chews a cud and has a four–part stomach, such as camels, cattle, sheep, and goats

savanna: a flat grassland with scattered trees, usually in a dry, warm climate

species: a group of animals of the same kind that can mate and produce similar offspring

ungulate: any animal with hoofs, such as goats, sheep, horses, and elephants

BOOKS

Arnold, Caroline. *Giraffe.* New York: William Morrow and Company, 1987.

Conklin, Gladys. *Giraffe Lives in Africa.* New York: Holiday House, 1971.

Denis-Huot, Christine and Michel. *The Giraffe: a Living Tower.* Watertown, MA: Charlesbridge, 1993.

Lepthien, Emilie. *Giraffes.* New York: Children's Press, 1996.

Leslie-Melville, Betty & Daisy Rothschild: *The Giraffe That Lives With Me.* New York: Bantam Doubleday Dell Publishing Group, 1987.

Sattler, Helen Roney. *Giraffes: The Sentinels of the Savannas.* New York: Lothrop, Lee and Shepaerd, 1989.

Switzer, Merebeth. *Giraffes.* Danbury, CT: Grolier Educational Corporation, 1988.

Wexo, John Bonnett. *Giraffes.* Mankato, Minnesota: Creative Education, 1991.

WEBSITES

Giraffes
http:// monterey.harrison.k12.co.us/Links/Af_Anim.htm

Nature–Wildlife Giraffe Page
http:// www.nature–wildlife.com/gir00.html

Seaworld Animal Bytes
http://www.seaworld.org/animal_bytes/giraffeab.html

Giraffes
http://www.wildlifesafari.org/giraffe.htm

Cheyenne Mountain Zoo
http://www.cmzoo.org/zoocam.html

ABOUT THE AUTHOR

Judith Jango–Cohen taught science for ten years before she started writing books. She learns about the animals she writes about by exploring in national parks. On her travels Judith takes along her husband Eliot, and her two children, Jennifer and Steven. Although she enjoys writing about animals, her family does not have any pets. Her children, however, hope to change that.

Page numbers in **boldface** are illustrations.